SACRED RIGHTS

FAITH LEADERS ON TOLERANCE AND RESPECT

*A special publication compiled by the Millennium World Peace Summit
of Religious and Spiritual Leaders in cooperation with the
Offices of the United Nations High Commissioner for Human Rights
to commemorate the World Conference against Racism,
Racial Discrimination, Xenophobia, and Related Intolerance*

**Durban, South Africa
August 31st—September 7th, 2001**

Photography by David Finn

Copyright ©2001 The Millennium World Peace Summit
Photographs Copyright ©David Finn

This book was made possible by generous grants from the
Office of the United Nations High Commissioner for Human Rights,
the Modi Foundation, the Museum of World Religions,
and Sri Pramukh Singhji Sahib S.S. Manchanda in devotion
to His Holiness Sat Guru Jagjit Singhji Maharaj.

Published by Millwood Publishing.
All rights reserved. No part of the contents of this
book may be reproduced without the written consent
of the publisher.

Design by Barbara Berasi.
Printed by Expedi Printing Inc.
412 West 14th Street
New York, New York 10014

Millwood Publishing
301 East 57th Street
New York, New York 10022
U.S.A.

ISBN: 0-9640952-4-6

Cover photo: Sculpture by Michelangelo

TABLE OF CONTENTS

v
Preface
by **Bawa Jain**, *Secretary-General, Millennium World Peace Summit of Religious and Spiritual Leaders*

vii
Foreword
by **Dr. Bhupendra Kumar Modi**, **Venerable Dharma Master Hsin Tsao**, *and* **Sri Pramukh Singhji Sahib S.S. Manchanda** *in devotion to* **His Holiness Sat Guru Jagjit Singhji Maharaj**

ix
Introduction
by **Mary Robinson**, *United Nations High Commissioner for Human Rights*

Statements
by Religious Leaders

His Holiness Patriarch Alexy II	*2*
Her Holiness Sri Sri Mata Amritanandamayi Devi	*4*
His Holiness Aram I	*6*
His All Holiness Ecumenical Patriarch Bartholomew	*8*
His Excellency Alhaji Ado Bayero	*10*
His Grace Reverend George Carey	*12*

His Excellency Dr. Mustafa Ceric	14
His Holiness Swami Dayananda Saraswati	16
His Excellency Mufti Sheikh Ravil Gainutdin	18
Honorable Ela Gandhi	20
Venerable Samdech Preah Maha Ghosananda	22
Reverend Billy Graham	24
His Holiness Tenzin Gyatso	26
Reverend Jesse Jackson	28
Her Holiness Dadi Janki	30
His Holiness Shri Jayendra Saraswati	32
Honorable Coretta Scott King	34
His Excellency Sheikh Ahmed Kuftaro	36
The Most Reverend Izu Kudo	38
Chief Rabbi Israel Meir Lau	40
Dr. Albert Lincoln	42
Sri Daya Mata	44
Reverend Bishop Vashti M. McKenzie	46
Reverend Nichiko Niwano	48
His Grace Reverend Njongonkulu Ndungane	50
Dastur Dr. Jehangir Oshidari	52
His Holiness Pope John Paul II	54
His Holiness Abune Paulos	56
The Reverend Dr. Konrad Raiser	58
Chief Rabbi Jonathan Sacks	60
Venerable Sheng-Yen	62
His Excellency Dr. L. M. Singhvi	64
Rabbi Adin Steinsaltz	66
Chief Jake Swamp	68
His Excellency Dr. Abdullah bin Abdul Muhsin Al Turki	70
Wakatel Utiw/Wondering Wolf/Cirilo Alejandro Perez Oxlaj	72
Venerable Eshin Watanabe	74
His Excellency Sheikh Fawzi al-Zafzaf	76

79
Appendix
Biographies of Religious Leaders

PREFACE

On August 28th, 2000, more than 1,000 religious leaders from 110 countries, representing the world's major religions and faiths, gathered in the United Nations General Assembly Hall for the Millennium World Peace Summit of Religious and Spiritual Leaders. A key objective of the Summit was to encourage religious leaders to exert greater influence on reconciliation, healing and forgiveness in areas of armed conflict and tension, and to foster an attitude of respect for the diversity of the human family. The Summit was a critical first step: the journey still lies ahead of us.

In an era of rapid globalization, people who would live and act from a foundation of faith confront a critical challenge: not only to accept diversity of belief as a seminal human right, but to work for its enactment on a global scale. Passive appreciation is good but insufficient for building societies free of intolerance.

Every religious tradition teaches mutual respect to treat one's neighbor as oneself regardless of racial, religious, ethnic, national, economic, age or gender differences. Between the teaching and rightful behavior, however, lies a great psychological chasm. We fear that which we do not understand. Religious leaders at the Summit consequently renewed their commitment to actively foster ethical and spiritual values in their respective communities. Now comes the work of establishing this commitment as part of the collective human ethic. The United Nations World Conference against Racism, Racial Discrimination, Xenophobia and Related Intolerance is a major step forward in seeing this commitment honored by the world's civic and political leaders.

Racism, particularly in the form of religious discrimination, is one of the main causes of violence. In many regions, distrust of religious differences is used as the rallying point for violence. Yet no religion teaches violence, and those who follow the spiritual path can and must play a key role in healing divisions by focusing on what is common to us all. Religion in its deepest sense enables people to perceive their kinship with others. Practiced purely, it is the foundation of our common humanity. We have asked our religious leaders to take a stand against prejudice and intolerance, and their response is reflected in the statements of grace and wisdom presented in this book. High Commissioner of Human Rights Mary Robinson and her staff have worked tirelessly toward this goal and deserve our deepest appreciation. A special thanks is due as well to the staff of Ruder Finn and the Millennium World Peace Summit for their sensitivity and dedication to seeing the book through to completion.

Bawa Jain

Secretary-General, Millennium World Peace Summit of Religious and Spiritual Leaders

The battle against racism and intolerance must engage all sectors of society to be effective. Religious leaders provide moral authority to the call for people to live with respect and understanding for differences. Government enacts laws to protect people against discrimination, but ultimately it is up to civil society to implement this moral imperative. Business has a role to play, and it is for this reason that Ruder Finn has committed itself to the work of the Millennium World Peace Summit and is supporting this initiative of the United Nations High Commissioner for Human Rights to promote tolerance and respect for all. It is of the utmost urgency that societies around the world renew the moral and spiritual commitment to live in peace, to treat all people with dignity and to honor the diversity that enriches and gives great beauty to the human community.

Dena Merriam

Office of the Chair, the Ruder Finn Group Vice-Chair, the Millennium World Peace Summit

FOREWORD

As boundaries separate countries and yet the world is one family, so we humans are separated by differences and yet humanity is one. If we see this, then duality fades and we rejoice in the diversity that fills God's creation. The time has come to see differences as the common trait that unifies us. That is the role played by the world's many religious traditions: to provide the spiritual lens through which the underlying unity of all people is revealed. This collection of statements by distinguished religious leaders challenges us to look deeper into the heart of our own religious culture and of those that surround us. If this book helps move us in this critical direction, then my modest contribution is fulfilled. I am deeply grateful to those who have brought such inspiring words together.

Dr. Bhupendra Kumar Modi

The Modi Foundation

We are here to contribute, each of us in our own humble way, to uniting the human family. Historically the human family has been separated by fear of differences, by intolerance toward the very gift that is our greatest resource. Differences enrich us. My hope for Buddhist children is that they learn the beauty of Judaism, Christianity, Islam, and Hinduism. This small volume reveals that beauty through the words of faith leaders and the creative inspiration of artists through the ages. May we all take inspiration from the words and images we find here, and may that inspiration empower our work of uniting our most wonderful and diverse human family.

Venerable Dharma Master Hsin Tsao

The Museum of World Religions

For Sikhs, B*hakti* or devotion to God, is the highest goal of human life. But how can devotion be achieved if one thinks himself better than any other being? Love starts with humility, as Guru Nanak Sahib says, "When the dirt of falsehood vanishes and life is pure and clean." To achieve such a state of humble devotion, the man of God rejects all prejudice. Sri Satguru Ram Singhji firmly believed that world peace can be achieved only through nonviolence. His Holiness Sat Guru Jagjit Singhji Maharaj wishes this timely conference all success.

Sri Pramukh Singhji Sahib S.S. Manchanda,
in devotion to **His Holiness Sat Guru Jagjit Singhji Maharaj**

Namdhari International Trust

INTRODUCTION

Religion and faith remain powerful guides to good conduct and moral action, often running deeper than Law and State which, in the grand sweep of history, are relatively new institutions. For millennia, sacred values have bound together members of communities in a spirit of solidarity and continue to bring people closer together. Regrettably, religion has also been used as a pretext to separate communities and stoke the embers of distrust and suspicion, sometimes with tragic consequences.

Yet, as Bishop Desmond Tutu pointed out in a Special Debate in the UN Commission on Human Rights on the subject of Tolerance and Respect, "no religion could hope to have a monopoly on God, on goodness and virtue and truth." Article 18 of the Universal Declaration of Human Rights affirms that "Everyone has the right to freedom of thought, conscience and religion; this right includes freedom to change his religion or belief, and freedom, either alone or in community with others and in public or private, to manifest his religion or belief in teaching, practice, worship and observance."

As globalization makes the world smaller, people of all faiths are coming together to recognize common values and to view their differences as productive elements in a dialogue and exchange of experiences, rather than as threats to be feared. In this sense, the infinite variety displayed in the human character is reflected in the diverse forms and manifestations of universal values—most of all in the respect for human rights standards and the dignity of the human being. Indeed, this is the philosophy and spirit behind the "Declaration on Tolerance and Diversity: A Vision for the 21st Century" which President Thabo

Mbeki of South Africa and I launched in New York during the Millennium Assembly last September and which has so far attracted the signatures of over 75 Heads of State. The Declaration emphasizes that, in order to eradicate racism, racial discrimination, xenophobia, and related intolerance, it is not enough only to fight against these evils. Rather, it is incumbent upon each one of us to strive towards the positive fulfillment of our shared vision for an inclusive, nonracial, and nondiscriminatory world so that, together, we may develop and guard rights sacred to all.

It is also the spirit behind the present volume which brings together statements of religious leaders from around the world at the dawn of a new millennium. 2001 is the year of the World Conference against Racism, Racial Discrimination, Xenophobia, and Related Intolerance and the International Year of Mobilization against Racism, Racial Discrimination, Xenophobia and Related Intolerance, as well as the Year of Dialogue among Civilizations. I welcome this volume as an important contribution to the promotion of mutual respect among people of all faiths and religions and the universal understanding that all human rights are sacred rights.

Mary Robinson

*United Nations High Commissioner for Human Rights
and Secretary General of the World Conference against Racism,
Racial Discrimination, Xenophobia, and Related Intolerance*

STATEMENTS
by Religious Leaders

Overcoming racial and ethnic intolerance today is a vitally important task for humanity in general and many individual societies in particular. I appreciate the efforts of the United Nations in this area.

It is my conviction that enmity and hatred can be overcome only if opposition to them will be accompanied with efforts to build a just world order and to rectify contradictions existing in political, economic, and social areas.

It has to be stated with bitterness that racism, xenophobia, and ethnic intolerance do manifest themselves in the world today. For the last decade we have become witnesses to numerous inter-ethnic conflicts, including those in the territory of the Commonwealth of Independent States and the Baltics. The Russian Orthodox Church has always raised its voice in the defense of victims of violence and in support of reconciliation, reminding people of the words of Holy Scriptures: "Depart from evil, and do good; seek peace, and pursue it" (Ps 34:14). We exert all possible efforts to prevent conflict situations. The faithful of our Church are well aware how difficult it is to achieve success in peacemaking. Therefore, they are appreciative of any initiative directed to overcoming strife, hatred, and violence. The idea of tolerance combined with commitment to moral principles is best expressed in the words of Christ the Saviour: "Whatever you wish that men would do to you, do so to them" (Mt. 7:12).

His Holiness Patriarch Alexy II

Patriarch of Moscow and of All Russia

SCULPTURE BY DANIEL CHESTER FRENCH

Depart from evil, and do good;
seek peace, and pursue it.

We have started the new millennium with great hopes and expectations of change. The inner change must happen within our selves. For only when conflict and negativity are removed from within, can we truly constitute a role in establishing peace. The very words "nation" and "religion" imply division and diversity. This diversity may seem to create obstacles in fostering peace, happiness, and prosperity in the world. Yet, just as a bouquet made of flowers with a variety of colors is more beautiful than a bouquet of flowers that are exactly the same, it is human diversity that brings richness and beauty to the world and human life.

There is one truth that shines through the creation of all mountains, plants, animals, the sun, the moon and the stars. You and I, all are expressions of this one reality. It is by assimilating this truth in our lives and thus gaining a deeper understanding that we can discover the inherent beauty in this diversity.

Her Holiness Sri Sri Mata Amritanandamayi Devi
Hindu Spiritual Leader

Just as a bouquet made of flowers with a variety of colors is more beautiful
than a bouquet of flowers that are exactly the same,
it is human diversity that brings richness and beauty
to the world and human life.

Intolerance has become the mark of many contemporary societies. The causes for intolerance are economic, religious, social, and political. Intolerance is evil; it is a source of violence, hatred, and division, and it manifests itself through racism, discrimination, xenophobia, and violation of human rights. Therefore, it must be eradicated in human societies. Religions, actors of civil societies and states can together play a pivotal role in combating violence in all its forms and expressions. I consider such a partnership of crucial importance in this globalized world—a partnership that maintains the particularities of each individual, uplifts the specific vocations of each, and strengthens collaboration for common action.

For all people of faith, eradication of intolerance is a continual affirmation of their own beliefs and religious values. For Christians it is a response to the will of God. As the Spiritual Head of the Armenian Catholicosate of Cilicia, and the Moderator of the Central Committee of the World Council of Churches, I pray that the growing partnership between the United Nations, world religions, and civil society will become real, and that this effort to work together will deepen collaboration on issues arising from intolerance and give shape to relevant forms of action in concrete situations. It is also my hope that the forthcoming Durban World Conference will wrestle with the question of intolerance seriously and responsibly, that its message will touch the conscience of all those who perpetrate human rights violations, and commit all people of good faith to go beyond mere statements and actually make a difference. I hope and pray that all of these things happen not for our own glory but for the Glory of the Creator and the integrity of His creation.

His Holiness Aram 1

Catholicos of the Great House of Cilicia, Catholicosate Armenian

SCULPTURE BY ANTONIO CANOVA

Religions can together play a pivotal role in combating violence in all its forms and expressions. I consider such a partnership of crucial importance in this globalized world—a partnership that **maintains the particularities of each individual**, uplifts the specific vocations of each, and strengthens collaboration for common action.

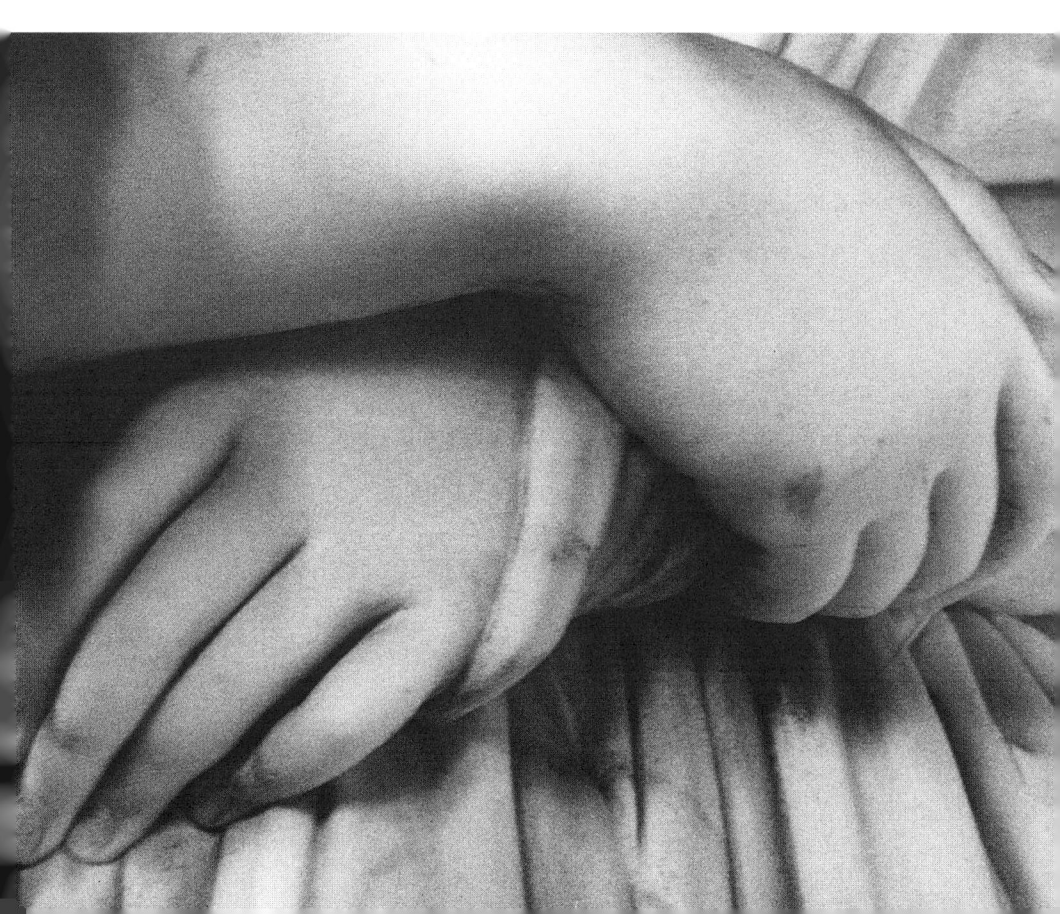

Whenever human beings fail to recognize the value of diversity, they deeply diminish the glory of God's creation. Following the example of the three persons of the Holy Trinity—the Father, the Son, and the Holy Spirit—all human beings are called to exist relationally to one another, united in the bond of love, as different and unique persons, each endowed with specific talents and characteristics, each created in the image and likeness of God. All human beings—regardless of religion, race, national origin, color, creed, or gender—are living icons of God, innately worthy of such respect and dignity. Whenever human beings fail to treat others with this respect, they insult God, the Creator, as is explained in the teachings of the Christian Scriptures.

Orthodox Christians throughout the world live side by side with peoples of other religions. With the rapid rise of advancement in communication and mobility, human beings are increasingly liberated from the geographical boundaries that used to separate them. As a result of recast boundaries, people now find themselves living in a global village amidst new neighbors who represent widely differing world perspectives, histories, and cultures. The realities of pluralism challenge each person in the global village to reflect more critically upon the teachings of his or her own faith, in light of the multitude of differing perspectives. An Orthodox Christian responds to these challenges with the understanding that we must always be tolerant of the perspectives of others, especially when such perspectives differ on the basis of religious, cultural, or historical ideology.

Amen.

His All Holiness Ecumenical Patriarch Bartholomew

Archbishop of Constantinople, New Rome and Ecumenical Patriarch

ALL HUMAN BEINGS—REGARDLESS OF RELIGION, RACE, NATIONAL ORIGIN, COLOR, CREED, OR GENDER—ARE LIVING ICONS OF GOD, INNATELY WORTHY OF RESPECT AND DIGNITY.

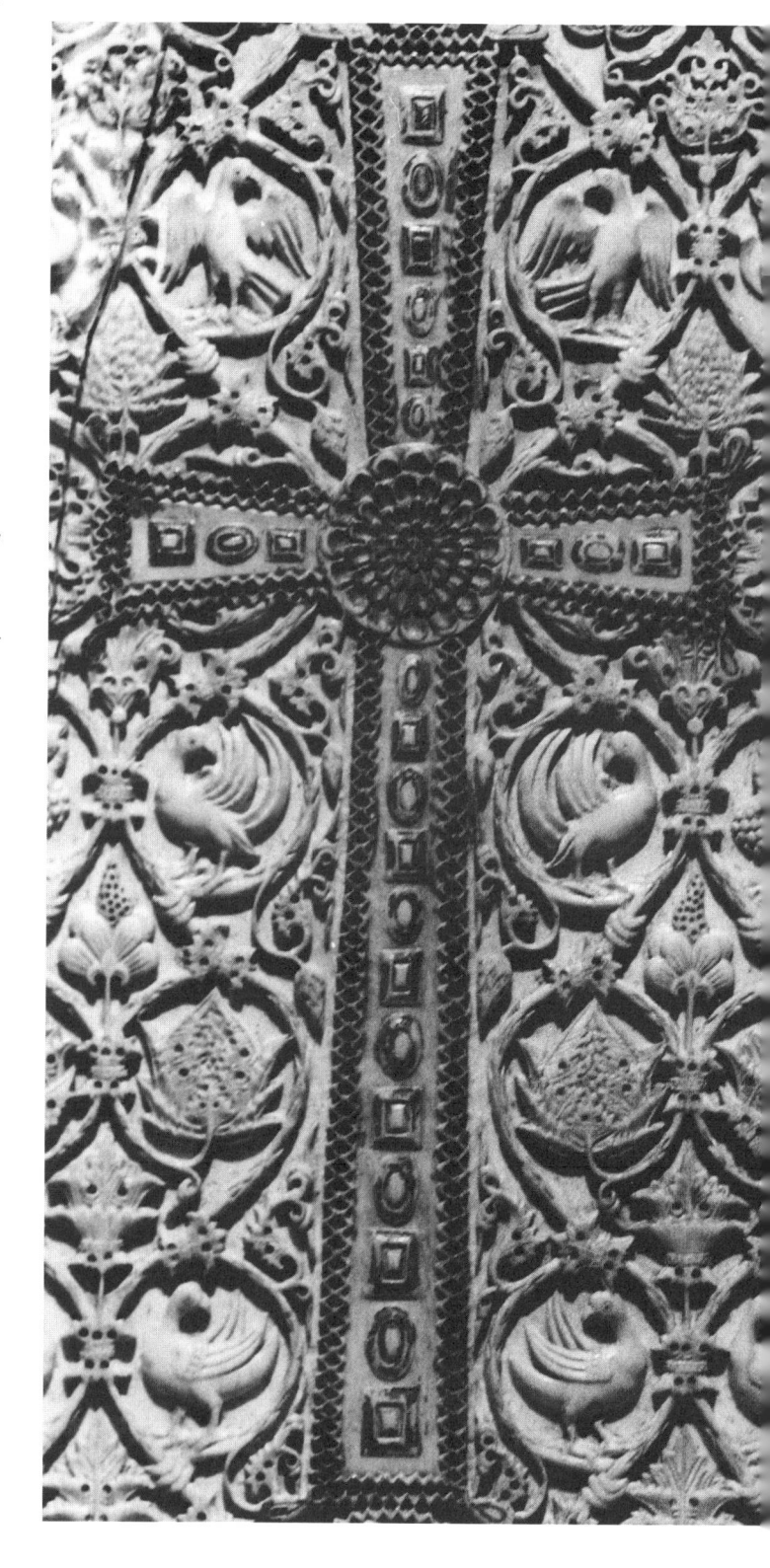

Islam as a religion and culture arose in order to eradicate the evils and social ills that bedevil the world. These evils include racial discrimination, as well as economic and political exploitation. To this end, Islam has always been a religion of peace, tolerance, and a system of beliefs that has been calling on man to understand his fellow human beings and accord respect to one another. In fact, the word *Islam*, meaning "submission to the will of God," also connotes "peace." Islam has recognized the rights not only of human beings but also the rights of animals and plants to exist without any hindrance.

Ameen.

His Excellency Alhaji Ado Bayero

The Emir of Kano, Nigeria

PAINTED PANEL, MOROCCO

Islam has recognized the rights not only of human beings but also the rights of animals and plants to exist without any hindrance.

Tolerance and the acceptance of diversity lie at the heart of the Anglican Christian tradition. Anglican Christians throughout the world see in this celebration of diversity and commitment to tolerance a reflection of our understanding of God and His love for humankind.

These are not easy virtues and they constantly recall us to faithfulness to the God whom we serve.

As Archbishop of Canterbury, I welcome any initiative that brings the World's Faith Communities together to combat the intolerance which has brought so much misery to our world.

His Grace Reverend George Carey
Archbishop of Canterbury

Anglican Christians throughout the world
see in this celebration of
diversity and commitment to tolerance
a reflection of our understanding of God
and His love for humankind.

In the name of God,
the compassionate,
the merciful

My Lord,
Teach me that tolerance is the highest
degree of strength
and the desire for revenge
the first sign of weakness.

My Lord,
If you deprive me of my property,
leave me hope.
If you grant me success,
grant me also the willpower
to overcome defeat.
And when you take away the blessing
of health,
grant me the blessing of faith.

My Lord,
When I sin against people,
grant me the power to ask for forgiveness,
and when people harm me,
then grant me the power to forgive.

My Lord,
If I forget you,
do not forget me.

Amen!

His Eminence Dr. Mustafa Ceric
Raisu-I-Ulama of Bosnia-Herzegovina

METALWORK, MOROCCO

tolerance is the **highest degree** of **strength**
and the **desire** for **revenge**
the **first sign** of **weakness.**

If recent biological discoveries are true, there is no biological basis for difference among races. All human beings are the same. If the differences are true, they only make humanity colorful. It does not call for any complex or discrimination. In fact, our reverence for life has to include every living organism and extend further to cover the entire universe.

The Upanisads tell us *Isavasyam idam sarvam*—"all that is here should be looked on as the manifestation of Isvara, God." The Hindu prayer is *lokas-samastas-sukhino bhavantu*—"may all be happy."

The Bhagavad Gita (12.13) defines a mature person as one who is *adveshta sarvabhutanam maitrah karuna eva ca*—"one who is totally free from hatred towards all beings and whose love and compassion encompass all beings."

His Holiness Swami Dayananda Saraswati

Sanskrit and Vedanta Scholar

our reverence for life has to include *every living organism* and extend further to cover *the entire universe.*

The Muslims of Russian Federation represent a part of the Islamic world that promotes tolerance and respect in every nation. We never agree with racial discrimination and unequal human rights.

We, as a minority within all nations of Russia, are determined to promote understanding, tolerance, and respect in matters relating to racism, racial discrimination, and xenophobia, and support all U.N. initiatives to eradicate these injustices.

We follow the law of life as exemplified by the words of the Koran: "God bestowed dignity upon us." In accordance with the Fickh, the Testament of Mohammed reads, "all persons enjoy the same rights." Our aim is to promote and practice peace, love, and unity among the people of the world.

His Excellency Mufti Sheikh Ravil Gainutdin

Chairman, Council of All Muftis of Russia

CEILING LAMP, MOROCCO

THE TESTAMENT OF MOHAMMED READS:
"all persons enjoy the same rights". Our aim is to promote and practice peace, love, and unity among the people of the world.

I have been greatly inspired by the teachings of Gandhiji, who writes of one Supreme Lord. For me, therefore, there is but one God or Infinite Power. The different faiths are but different paths to the same end. We may have different features, we may have different complexions and hair texture, we may speak different languages, we may be male, female, or of different sexual orientations, we may worship in different ways, we may be rich or poor—but our humanity remains consistently the same. The sooner we realize this important message, the sooner we will be able to save mankind from a painful and horrendous doom—a doom of war and of natural disasters as a result of the excessive use of armaments of all types and the resultant destruction of nature.

I believe that those who do not believe in God but believe in values because they love and respect humanity, mother earth, and all its creatures, deserve equal respect and recognition, just as in the story of the good Samaritan in the Holy Bible. Similar examples are found in every scripture where a non-believer proves his humanity by his noble deeds and God loves him for these noble deeds.

We need to interpret our scriptures so that our value systems are enhanced, our beliefs in ourselves and our fellow creatures are enhanced, and so that we begin to show greater respect to mother earth and her creations. If we are to survive another millennium, then man has to heed the signs of foreboding coming from the melting ice of the north.

Honorable Ela Gandhi

Member of Congress, South Africa,
Granddaughter of Mahatma Gandhi

DANCING DEVATA, INDIA

*We need to interpret our scriptures so that **our value systems are enhanced, our beliefs in ourselves and our fellow creatures are enhanced,** and so that we begin to **show greater respect to mother earth and her creations.***

Peacemaking requires the skill of listening. To listen, we have to give up ourselves, even our own words. We listen until we can hear our own peaceful nature. As we learn to listen to ourselves, we learn to listen to others as well, and new ideas of peace grow up within us. There is an openness, a harmony, as we come to trust one another. We discover new possibilities for resolving conflicts, for ending our fighting with one another. When we listen well, we will hear the birth of peace.

Peacemaking requires mindfulness. There is no peace with jealousy, self-righteousness or meaningless criticism. We must decide that making peace is more important than making war.

Peacemaking requires self-peace. There is little we can do for peace as long as we feel that we are the only ones that know the way. A real peacemaker will strive only for peace, not for fame, for glory, for name, or even for honor. Striving for fame, glory, or honor will only harm our efforts. We must be open to others, sharing peace with them. Only then will we know peace in ourselves.

Venerable Samdech Preah Maha Ghosananda

Supreme Patriarch of Cambodia

peacemaking requires mindfulness.

Today we are privileged to live in an age marked by dramatic advancements in global transportation, technology, and communications. These trends have already brought many benefits to the human race, and will almost certainly accelerate as we move into the 21st century.

Like most developments in human history, however, the shrinking barriers of our time also have had a negative side, opening the door to new levels of racism, intolerance, terrorism, and violence. More than ever, the moral and spiritual leaders of our world must stand together against every evil that threatens the peace and dignity of any human being.

Those of us who are Christians affirm that all humans are created in the image of God, and God's love extends equally to every person on earth, regardless of race, tribe, or ethnic origin. As our Holy Bible affirms, God "gives all men life and breath and everything else. From one man He made every nation of men, that they should inhabit the whole earth;...so that men would seek Him" (Acts 17:25-27). We further believe that Jesus' supreme act of sacrifice demonstrated with finality God's determination to bring into His eternal Kingdom those "from every tribe and language and people and nation" (Revelation 5:9).

Every act of discrimination and racism, therefore, is wrong, and is a sin in the eyes of God. This is why Jesus commanded His followers to become peacemakers, saying, "Blessed are the peacemakers, for they will be called sons of God" (Matthew 5:9).

Reverend Billy Graham

SCULPTURE BY VERROCCHIO

Every act of discrimination and racism, therefore, is wrong, and is a sin in the eyes of God.

In recent history, our world has become smaller and more interdependent. Political and economic ties, linked by worldwide communications, unite us. However, we are also drawn together by problems: overpopulation, dwindling natural resources, and an environmental crisis that threatens the very existence of the planet.

Within the context of this new interdependence, self-interest clearly lies in considering the interests of others. We must develop a greater sense of universal responsibility. Each of us must learn to work not just for our own self, family, or nation, but also for the benefit of all humankind.

Love and compassion are the ultimate source of joy and happiness. Once we recognise their value and actually try to cultivate them, many other good qualities—forgiveness, tolerance, inner strength, and confidence—come forth naturally. These qualities are essential if we are to create a better, happier, more stable, and civilized world.

Of course, human beings naturally possess different interests and dispositions. So, it is not surprising that we have many different systems of belief and different ways of thinking and behaving. And this variety is a way for everyone to be happy. If we have a great variety of food, we will be able to satisfy everyone's diverse tastes and needs. When we only have bread, the people who eat rice are left out.

The more we understand one another's ways, the more we can learn from each other. And the more easily we can develop respect and tolerance in our own lives and in our behavior towards each other. This will certainly help to increase peace and friendship throughout the world.

His Holiness Tenzin Gyatso

XIV Dalai Lama

self-interest *clearly lies in considering the* **interests of others.**

If the central problem of the 20th century was the color line, then the imperative for the 21st century is to eliminate the gap between surplus culture and deficit culture. Globally, too few control too much, at the expense of too many.

One manifestation of the global imbalance of resources is the perpetuation of "isms" around the world, known to most as racism, sexism, and totalitarianism. Racism, for example, was a political construct from the beginning, designed to exploit physiological differences between the peoples of the earth by ranking them (in a linear manner) to correspond privilege, poverty, and punishment with skin color or birth status. There is no scientific basis for race. Contrary to historical and scientific evidence, darker-skinned people's contribution to human civilization has often been stamped "inferior" and they are regarded as a "minority." But whether black, brown, red, or white, we are all precious in God's sight. Justice should not be dispensed on the basis of black or white, but rather wrong or right.

After all, what is the benefit of hate? If one is a harbinger of hate, rational thought is diminished, thereby limiting the desired outcome. Hate just does not make sense.

Keep Hope Alive!

Reverend Jesse Jackson
Founder, Rainbow/PUSH Foundation

SCULPTURE BY EDNA MANLEY

Whether black, brown, red, or white...

we are all precious in God's sight.

If nothing else, I should be able to do one thing in my life, and that is to know how to stay happy. Tolerance makes happiness possible; and, in turn, happiness increases tolerance. Tolerance is a way of being and behaving that naturally brings me dignity and upholds the dignity of others. The compassion and love that tolerance brings to my relationships enables me to experience true happiness. In fact, my inner happiness should keep on increasing to such an extent that if someone comes along to steal it, I have so much to share that they too become happy! God doesn't want me to have worries; God wants me to be happy.

Someone who has tolerance won't even say "I have to tolerate," because that implies they are feeling sorrow. Instead, they will say, "It's not a problem. There is something for me to learn in this." Whatever the situation, tolerance enables me to learn. Perhaps I need patience, or humility, or understanding. Tolerance allows my peace and my love to stay constant. That way, I stay connected with the Source of all that is good, so that I can help both myself and others.

Tolerance enables me to stay focused, so I can be connected with God, and the light that comes from that connection enables me to see what I need to do at every moment, and how to do it. Chaos may surround me, but if I have that light in front of me, I know where to go. If I experience that light in each step I take, then I can illuminate the way for others as well.

Her Holiness Dadi Janki
Brahma Kumaris Spiritual Leader

Tolerance
is a way
of being
and behaving
that naturally
brings me dignity
and upholds
the dignity
of others.

Every human being should feel love and affection toward others. Nowadays many people keep pet-animals in their houses and near them with love. But man is not responding to humans in the same way. Man uses his knowledge to develop science and technology, but not to develop a loving mood toward his neighbors. If man were truly wise, he would cultivate knowledge that allowed him to develop compassion toward fellow human beings. Human society consists of crores of humans. Man should understand that as he enjoys/suffers the joys/problems of life, everyone else in society also experiences the same things. Man should see every other human as he sees himself. Only through such a broad vision will human society take a correct path and receive the blessings of the Almighty.

His Holiness blesses the conference with all success.

His Holiness Shri Jayendra Saraswati
Sri Sankaracharyaji Kanchi Kamakoti Peetadhipathi

If man were truly wise, he would cultivate knowledge that allowed him to ***develop compassion*** toward fellow human beings.

The specter of racism has haunted humanity throughout world history. Genocide, slavery, and tribal warfare have claimed the lives of millions through the centuries. Many more have suffered the cruel ravages of racial segregation and discrimination. In the 21st century, we must eradicate this terrible scourge from the earth.

Although racism has been thoroughly institutionalized in many societies, seemingly resisting any kind of reform, the American Civil Rights Movement and liberation struggles in Africa, India, and other places have taught us that it can be dismantled through the persistent, determined application of organized non-violence.

As a Christian minister, my husband, Martin Luther King, Jr., often affirmed the essential unity of all people. Martin called for "a worldwide fellowship that lifts neighborly concerns beyond one's tribe, race, class, and nation." He said that "an all-embracing and unconditional love for all" is "the supreme unifying principle of life." This Hindu-Muslim-Christian-Jewish-Buddhist belief about ultimate reality is beautifully summed up in the First Epistle of Saint John: "Let us love one another; for love is of God. And every one that loveth is born of God and knoweth God. He that loveth not, knoweth not God; for God is love...if we love one another, God dwelleth in us, and his love is perfected in us."

We can create the beloved community that Martin Luther King, Jr. envisioned. Let us now dare to embrace this common vision and mobilize all of our resources to bring a new era of healing and hope into being.

Honorable Coretta Scott King

Founder of the Martin Luther King Jr. Center for Nonviolent Social Change

SCULPTURE BY KARL BROODHAGAN

RACISM can be dismantled through the persistent, determined application of ORGANIZED NONVIOLENCE.

Islam makes it absolutely clear that all humanity is but one great family. The origin of all people is one, as all human beings were created from a single soul.

God says in the Holy Koran:
"O mankind, revere your Guardian-Lord Who created you from a single person, created of like nature [his] mate, and from them twain scattered countless men and women." (Holy Koran, Sura 4, verse 1).

As all people are part of the family of God, Islam insists that there should be absolute equality and respect between all human beings. The sole standard of value in Islam cannot be race, color, ethnicity, or privilege, but only righteousness. Prophet Muhammad condemned the maltreatment of any person on the grounds of color, race, or religion. He called people to regard the revealed religions with respect and commanded adherence to them by their respective followers. All this was done to create a productive human society in which the individual was favored on the basis of his piety, observance of duty, protection of rights, and avoidance of evil.

It is my earnest prayer that God the Almighty give us the power to act justly without any prejudice and work together indiscriminately towards that end.

His Excellency Sheikh Ahmed Kuftaro
Grand Mufti of Syria

CARVED ARCHWAY, MOROCCO

The sole standard of value in Islam
cannot be race, color,
ethnicity or privilege,
but only righteousness.

Venerating Tenno, as the performer of the divine will of Kami, Shinto followers should live in harmony and heartily pray for the prosperity of the country as well as for the coexistence and co-prosperity of peoples of the world. The expression of praying for such coexistence and co-prosperity, as found in the general principles of Shinto followers, shows an ideal way of life, one that Shintoists are asked to honor and with which they must comply. Thus, the Shinto mind-set completely denies any thoughts based on intolerance, racism, and xenophobia.

The Most Reverend Izu Kudo
President of the Association of Shinto Shrines

STANDING KWANNON FIGURE, JAPAN

The Shinto mind-set completely denies any thoughts based on intolerance, racism, and xenophobia.

Judaism not only educates towards tolerance and understanding between observant and non-observant Jews, but also believes in tolerance between Jews and other religions and peoples, because all of us, all of humanity, were created in one image, the image of the Creator of the Universe. We all have one Father, one God who created us.

The goal, however, is not to create a universal humanity and thus blur individual identity. Unity among religions and nations is desirable, but it is equally important to preserve the uniqueness of each people and religion. As the prophet Micah tells us in the Bible: "for let all peoples walk, each one in the name of its God, and we shall walk in the name of the Lord."

Every person who educates himself in this spirit—to preserve the identity of his people and religion while simultaneously respecting different and opposing views with tolerance and patience—will in this way contribute to imbuing the world with an atmosphere of peace, for the sake of all the earth's creatures.

Chief Rabbi Israel Meir Lau
Chief Rabbi of Israel

SCULPTURE BY MICHELANGELO

UNITY, among religions and nations is desirable, but it is equally important to preserve the **UNIQUENESS** of each people and religion.

More than a century ago, Bahá'u'lláh declared that humankind was entering a new era in its history when accelerating processes of unification would compel recognition that humanity is a single people with a common destiny. In appealing to humanity to accept the central truth of its oneness, and to set aside the barriers of race, religion, and nationality, which have been the principal causes of conflict throughout history, Bahá'u'lláh urges "...regard ye not one another as strangers. Ye are the fruits of one tree, and the leaves of one branch." There is, He said, no possibility of achieving world peace until the fundamental principle of unity has been accepted and given practical effect in the organization of society.

That human consciousness necessarily operates through an infinite diversity of individual minds and motivations detracts in no way from its essential unity. Indeed, it is precisely an inhering diversity that distinguishes unity from homogeneity or uniformity. Acceptance of the concept of unity in diversity, therefore, implies the development of a global consciousness, a sense of world citizenship, and a love for all of humanity. It induces every individual to realize that, since the body of humankind is one and indivisible, each member of the human race is born into the world as a trust of the whole. It further suggests that if a peaceful international community is to emerge, then the complex and varied cultural expressions of humanity must be allowed to develop and flourish, as well as to interact with one another in ever-changing patterns of civilization. "The diversity in the human family," the Bahá'í writings emphasize, "should be the cause of love and harmony, as it is in music where many different notes blend together in the making of a perfect chord."

Dr. Albert Lincoln

Secretary General, Bahá'í International Community

SCULPTURE BY GUSTAV VIGELAND

THAT HUMAN CONSCIOUSNESS NECESSARILY OPERATES THROUGH AN INFINITE DIVERSITY OF INDIVIDUAL MINDS AND MOTIVATIONS DETRACTS IN NO WAY FROM ITS ESSENTIAL UNITY.

Now more than ever we must accept the truth: This *is* one world. It is made up of all different kinds of people with all their multifarious physical appearances, mentalities, interests, motivations. In uniting these endlessly varied blossoms of human individuality there is one basic principle that threads all of us like a garland—and that is God. In His eyes, none is greater, none is lesser; we are all His children. God is not the least bit interested in where we were born, which religion we follow, or what color our skin is. But He does care about how we behave.

To forget self by seeking the higher Self means to look always to the good in people as well as to the good in yourself. Recognize and bring out the qualities of the higher Self—the divine qualities of the soul that reside within you and within everyone else. It is the practice of these basic principles of truth and right behavior—plus meditation on God—that gradually transforms the totality of man's character. Strive each day to express a little more of that love, that positive-mindeness, that cheerfulness, that undaunted courage which constitutes God's presence in our souls. Be a carrier of sunshine, a carrier of goodwill. Each and every one of us has that divine spark within. It rests with us to bring it out—for our own highest benefit, and that of our world.

We must enlarge our vision and do away with the boundaries of prejudices; they can no longer exist in the era of the new world that is being born. Forget the lower self by seeking the higher Self. Cease being so preoccupied with "me," "I," "mine," and begin to think in terms of doing good to others—including others in our circle of friendship, drawing the whole world in. What a beautiful thought this is!

Sri Daya Mata

President and Sangmata, Self Realization Fellowship

SCULPTURE BY BRUNO LUCCHESI

Cease being so preoccupied with **"me," "I," "mine,"** *and begin to think in terms of* **doing good to others**—*including others in our circle of friendship, drawing the whole world in.*

There are many things that divide us: different doctrines, different dogmas, different tenets, different belief systems. But if we search hard, I believe we will also find some common grounds in our differentness without violating the uniqueness of our belief systems. Now, in the 21st century, we can begin to uncover the things that bring us together rather than dwell on the things that tear us apart. We can respect each other's cultural differences without demeaning each other or disrespecting another's belief, understanding that the uniqueness doesn't make us inferior or superior to each other but makes us unique in our pursuit of God's understanding.

Religion can play an important role in nonviolence, in reconciliation, and in the soothing of conflict by taking our eyes off of self and putting them on those that surround us. It is possible for religion to take a stand beyond personal agendas and inspire one to take a look at the whole community. This is not the sole duty of one country, one nation, one sect, one group, but all of us are responsible for the wholeness of the world that we live in.

Reverend Bishop Vashti M. McKenzie
African Methodist Episcopal Church

SCULPTURE BY CORI FALK

if we search hard, I believe we will also find some **common grounds in our differentness** *without violating the uniqueness of our belief systems.*

The fundamental truth of the Buddha's teachings, "the dharma of transience," shows that everything in the world is constantly changing—nothing remains unchanged. Humans, too, are born, grow and eventually die.

The following words of Sakyamuni Buddha are recorded in the Dhammapada: "Difficult it is being born a human. Difficult it is for those for whom death is inevitable."

Thus, one can awaken to the value of life through the dharma of transience. This awakening leads one to realize how the lives of others are as sacred as one's own.

When one lives by this truth, one naturally abandons any form of discrimination and prejudice. Discriminating against others is nothing other than debasing one's own life.

The very meaning of religion involves revealing the wonder, sacredness, and value of life. In other words, the greatest significance of religion lies in the elimination of discrimination and prejudice against others.

Reverend Nichiko Niwano

President, Rissho Kosei-kai

STANDING BUDDHA, INDIA

The very meaning of religion involves revealing the
WONDER, SACREDNESS, **and** VALUE OF LIFE.

Even though we may acknowledge our equality and oneness in the sight of God, in order to live with diversity and to enjoy its riches, there is much healing to be done and, foremost, the healing of fears that lurk in the deepest recesses of our minds and hearts. We need to admit these fears in order to achieve unity in diversity and diversity in unity and to appreciate one another's giftedness. But sometimes it is our very giftedness that becomes a threat to others, and only our brokenness that unites us. One very clear Biblical example of such a threat is that of Saul and his jealousy of David, which in the end lost him his kingdom.

The only way to overcome fear is through a love that really wants the best for others. To look at those with different backgrounds and see them as God sees them. We are all one in His eyes. As St Paul said (in relation to the Church, but it applies equally to our international situation as globalisation has shown us), no one part of the body can say it has no need of another, for we are interdependent and inextricably bound to one another as a global community.

There is an old saying that if you want peace, work for justice. I believe that our greatest challenge as the world's religious leaders is to consistently remind our political and business counterparts that peace is not the absence of war or conflict. It is the presence of those conditions in society that ensure basics, such as food, shelter, clothing, access to health care, clean water, and education. Peace is about giving facility and nurturing a spirit of love.

His Grace Reverend Njongonkulu Ndungane

Archbishop of Cape Town

SCULPTURE BY GERTRUDE VANDERBILT WHITNEY

The only way to overcome fear

is through a love that really wants

the best for others.

The faith of all people, including we Zoroastrians, is based on the conviction that almighty God, the creator of the world and everything in the world, who is omnipotent and omniscient, has created all mankind equal and free. We believe that at the time of judgment, regardless of all superficial differences such as race, lineage, gender, skin color, language, etc., He will consider their deeds, and His criterion will be only what people have done in their worldly life and nothing else. Man's status in the eyes of God depends upon virtues—not upon blood and parentage, or skin. No divine religion accepts discrimination between human beings according to outward appearances.

In our sacred book Avesta, in the first paragraph of the Yasna 54, the prophet Ashu Zartosht (Zoroaster) says: "May that brotherhood and friendship for which we all wish come toward us… Everyone who acts and behaves according to the call of the conscience will be appropriately awarded, an award which everyone hopes to enjoy and Ahura Mazda has ordained for them."

Dastur Dr. Jehangir Oshidari

High Priest of Zoroastrianism (Iran)

SCULPTURE FROM THE ABBEY OF MOISSAC

Man's status in the eyes of God depends upon virtues—not blood and parentage or skin.

Today, the 21st of March, we celebrate the United Nations International Day for the Elimination of Racial Discrimination. This day also marks the beginning of a week of solidarity with all those who fight against that injustice.

The International Instruments which have been adopted, the World conferences and, in particular, the upcoming Conference which will take place in Durban (South Africa) in September of this year, constitute important stages on the path towards the affirmation of the fundamental equality and dignity of every person and towards a peaceful coexistence among peoples. Despite these efforts, millions of human beings do not yet see their "right of citizenship" recognized within the human family.

The Church unites itself with the commitment of those who defend human rights and feels itself in solidarity with all those who are victims of discrimination for racial, ethnic, religious, or social reasons. Spiritual and religious values, with their potential for renewal, effectively contribute to improving society. It is a duty for religious communities to unite themselves with the worthy action of governments and International Organizations in this area.

I wish therefore to repeat that no one is a foreigner in the Church and that all should feel at home there! To make the Church "a home and a school of communion" is a concrete response to the hopes for justice in the world today.

His Holiness Pope John Paul II

SCULPTURE BY GIANLORENZO BERNINI

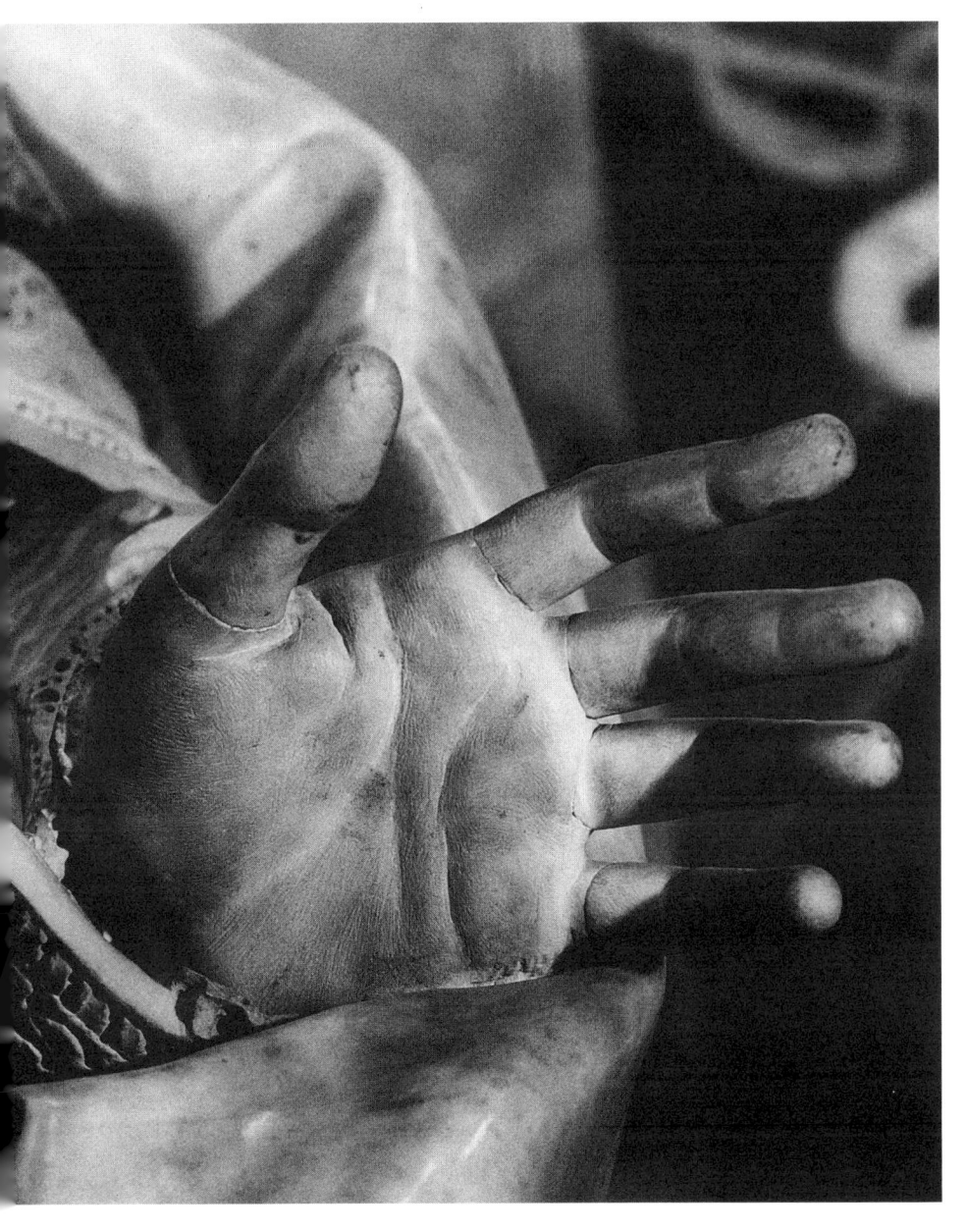

The Church unites itself with the commitment of those who defend human rights **and feels itself in solidarity** with all those who are victims of discrimination for racial, ethnic, religious, or social reasons.

Racism is an affront to human dignity because it belittles a fellow human being in the eyes of another. It is based on the erroneous notion that one race or color—black, brown, white, and so on— or having material possession, or political position, makes one superior to another. It demeans the God given human worth of a person.

We recall with a sense of profound sympathy, the atrocities committed and the countless injustices inflicted by one people against another throughout human history. Today more than ever, in this technologically advanced world, racial discrimination is widely and openly committed without shame in different ghastly forms throughout the world. In spite of the technological civilization attained by the world, it is disgraceful and shameful to see that racial discrimination is still being practiced everywhere daily. It is essential to note that all who have propagated and practiced racism have invariably met their doom.

Racial discrimination as an evil that detracts from the honor and dignity of a human being must be eliminated. It is our strong conviction that this could only be accomplished through accepting the Laws of God and recognizing our natural diversity. The evils of racial discrimination cannot be resolved through tolerance. Since tolerance itself implies recognizing racism and living with it, it doesn't aim at its eradication. Furthermore, diversity, which is a God given gift, must be wholeheartedly accepted and fully respected. And he that seriously observes the Divine dictate and guides his thinking and life accordingly does not commit an error as frivolous as racial discrimination. It is only when we miss the truth and apply our value judgments that we are led to such a fallacy. Rather, accepting and respecting our differences as a gift of God would go a long way in erasing our stereotyped views about each other.

His Holiness Abune Paulos

Patriarch of Ethiopia

SCULPTURE BY MAURICE GLICKMAN

accepting and respecting our differences
AS A GIFT OF GOD would go a long way in erasing our stereotyped views about each other.

In a religio-cultural ethos where social hierarchies were legitimized with philosophical imagery, St. Paul re-interprets the image of the body to uphold the spiritual significance of respecting the value and worth of every human being. He presents this image to emphasize the need to recognize diversity as an expression of God's wisdom and love, and calls for the need to be led by a spirituality that recognizes one's own worth in relation to the other. By drawing on the example of Christ, he offers a social vision embodied by the values of equality, justice, and love.

It is our hope that Christians around the world will join with peoples of other faiths in seeking to create a world free of the poverty and forms of discrimination that are at the root of violence. As I said at the Millennium World Peace Summit of Religious and Spiritual Leaders in New York last August, dialogue within and between religions must lead not only to tolerance but to deep respect for the other in his or her authentic relationship with the Holy. Together, we must seek ways to create a global culture of mutual respect which will provide a model to those who bear responsibility for governance at all levels of society, be it in the private, communal, or public spheres.

The Reverend Dr. Konrad Raiser

Secretary General, World Council of Churches

SCULPTURE BY MICHELANGELO

RELIGIONS MUST LEAD NOT ONLY TO TOLERANCE

BUT TO DEEP RESPECT FOR THE OTHER
IN HIS OR HER AUTHENTIC RELATIONSHIP
WITH THE HOLY.

In a world where we are consistently pressurized to consider crises and disaster, we the human guardians of our planet, must do all we can to ensure that no word or deed emanating from us aggravates existing differences. That, however, is but a preliminary and somewhat passive approach.

It is imperative that those who look to us for spiritual guidance and leadership are encouraged to examine, to understand, and to be tolerant of those points of view that may differ from our own but yet are sincerely held by others.

The words of the prophet Micah are as relevant to us today as when they were first uttered thousands of years ago.

"What does the Lord expect of you but to do justly, to love mercy, and to walk respectfully with your God."

Chief Rabbi Jonathan Sacks
Chief Rabbi of the Commonwealth

SCULPTURE BY LORENZO GHIBERTI

What does the Lord expect of you but to do justly, to love mercy, and to walk respectfully with your God.

No matter how many reasons are given, racism, racial discrimination, xenophobia, and intolerance are uncivilized and foolish actions. If we cannot recognize that the world is one family and the universe one whole, it will not only be devastating for ethnic minorities but may also precipitate a crisis that will lead to the destruction of our shared world.

This is truly a tragedy for humanity. It never occurs to most people that they could protect each other and collaborate to develop a wonderful future for everyone. Instead, they mercilessly kill and discriminate against one another, wasting humanity's resources.

Wasting humanity's resources means that, whether they are violent conflicts between primitive tribes or modern wars between nations and bloodshed between ethnic groups, such fights consume not only precious lives but also mental energy, time, and labor. People toil to produce and improve their living resources, but squander them on the destruction and devastation of wars. This all comes about due to people's foolish attitude. Thus, a wise people will certainly maintain a compassionate and sympathetic heart toward one another, and have limitless hope for the future and the ability to open up a broad space, where opposites attract.

From a Buddhist standpoint, opposites complement each other. In order to protect ourselves from other peoples who might take hostile action against us, and thus harm or inflict losses on us, we certainly must take steps for our self-protection. But the best way to protect ourselves is to transform our enemies into friends. And this is at the heart of Buddhist teaching.

Venerable Sheng-Yen

Buddhist Leader

HEAD OF BUDDHA, INDONESIA

the best way to protect ourselves is to transform our **enemies** into *friends*.

Tolerance is a state of mind, a set of norms and a pattern of behavior. It is another name for human understanding. It represents the spirit of openness. Its liberating influence on the human mind enhances human spirituality.

For many millennia, tolerance has been a way of life in India. The ancient Indic tradition, comprising the Vedic and the Sramana mainstreams, made tolerance the sheet anchor of society and civilization.

Tolerance was ingrained in the wisdom of the Vedas, the oldest surviving sacred scriptures of the world. The Vedic seers proclaimed thus: "Truth is One: many are the ways in which truth is perceived and interpreted."

The two main branches of the Sramana tradition, Jainism and Buddhism, elaborated on the concept of tolerance as the philosophical foundation of their faith traditions.

The Vedic and the Sramana traditions have had an uninterrupted history of tolerance through trackless centuries and is reflected in the outlook of the Indian People.

Tolerance is, in the ultimate analysis, the only way to unshackle humanity from egocentric pride and prejudice, from hatred and violence, from racial discrimination and religious fanaticism. Tolerance is the first and last bastion of human rights and human responsibilities. It is on the foundation of tolerant understanding that we can build the new edifice of reciprocity in human relationships, calling for universal love and friendship based on the recognition of human dignity and reverence for all life.

His Excellency Dr. L.M. Singhvi

Jain Scholar

HAND FROM STANDING BUDDHA, PAKISTAN

"Truth is One: many are the ways in which truth is perceived and interpreted."

The white-washing of differences is a mistake. Any attempt to take dissimilar things and make them similar is a big mistake. The notion of peace is the ability to unite differences, to live with those with whom I do not agree. There are many people whose theologies I don't agree with—but we can sit together, we can talk together, and we may create peace...and that's what I want to reach. It is not in making everybody equal and the same: not to cut all the heads to the same measure, but to keep us different and still like each other.

All of us believe, in one way or another, that humanity is—in one way or another—created in the image of God. We believe that there is a distinctiveness and a specialness about humankind. The rights of man are not derived from the United Nations declaration. The rights of man, the initial rights of man, come from the fact that all of us, whoever we are, low order or high, are born in the image of God. The divinity that is in us all deserves great honor.

Rabbi Adin Steinsaltz
Leading Talmudic Scholar

ARYEH STEINBERGER, SUKKAH, PAINTED CANVAS

The notion of **PEACE,**
is the ability to unite differences,
to live with those with whom
I do not agree.

Everywhere we go in the world today people are silently thinking "world peace." Peace is a very powerful ingredient in the human experience, especially if one has the ability to live it. Peace starts with the individual. One has to be disciplined, have inner security, and have the ability to practice justice with all their relations.

There is a prophesy among our Haudenosaunee people that has been handed down orally since the beginning of recorded time. It goes like this: At the very beginning, humans could not get along with one another. The great spirit was saddened by this and decided to send people in various directions to learn about themselves. The great spirit told them, the day will come when all of the world's children will come back together. The people will share the knowledge they have gained, and will be placed in a great bundle, which then, will be tied. The separation of the world's people cannot and should not continue.

There is a great need for the world's people to heal from the effects of war. The result of war is the displacement of people and the insecurity caused by grief. Grief causes tears to flow, and causes an inability to see the future. Grief causes deafness so that people no longer have the ability to hear one another. When grief becomes lodged in a person's throat, they no longer have the ability to speak with each other. For the tears, deafness, and loss of voice to be restored, there is a great need for humankind to show kindness, justice, and humility to each other. This is the ancient tradition of the Haudenosaunee.

Chief Jake Swamp

Wolf Clan of the Mohawk Nation, Six Nations Iroquois Federation

SCULPTURE BY ALLAN HOUSER

For the tears, deafness, and loss of voice to be restored, there is a great need for humankind to **show kindness, justice, and humility to each other**.

This is the tradition of the Haudenosaunee.

Islam, with its comprehensive teachings and principles, constitutes a complete code of life. It is a religion for all peoples and for all times and it manifests in various ways. Thus, no superiority is assigned to one nation over another or one people over another. Indeed, Islam emphatically abrogates all tribal, ethnic, and racial discrimination, and has established righteousness and virtue as the criteria for preference in society.

The prophet Muhammad (may Allah's peace and blessings be upon him) in his sermon on the Mount of Arafa during his last Hajj said: All mankind is from Adam and Eve. An Arab has no superiority over a non-Arab, nor does a non-Arab have any superiority over an Arab; also a white person has no superiority over a black person nor a black person over a white person, except by piety and good action.... Remember one day you will appear before God (the Creator) and you will answer for your deeds.

The Muslim World League reminds the world that if the human family is to survive and prosper we must remove prejudice and discrimination and its corollary, injustice, from our lives—for there can be no harmony and peace without justice and no justice without mutual respect.

His Excellency Dr. Abdullah bin Abdul Muhsin Al Turki
Secretary General, World Muslim League

*...there can be no harmony and peace
without JUSTICE...*

*and no JUSTICE
without mutual respect.*

Greetings to the world!

The Indigenous people of the Americas raise their voices to the Heavens with a cry: no more contamination, no more racial discrimination, no more violence; we are all brothers and sisters, we all have equal value, like flowers of one garden. We all have one Creator, one sun that illuminates us all and gives us warmth; one air—the same air that we all breathe and which gives life, from the first breath to our last; one water—we all drink the same water that mitigates our thirst and converts into blood in our bodies; and only one Mother Earth that holds us and feeds us all.

Exploitation and racism are responsible for the destruction and contamination of the environment, exterminating forests, animals, and minerals.

The Indigenous People of America raise their voices to the heavens: no more racial discrimination, no more contamination, no more violence. No more nuclear testing. Think about your children and future generations.

The Prophecy of the Maya tells us:
"Arise. All arise, not one nor two groups be left behind."

Wakatel Utiw/Wondering Wolf/Cirilo Alejandro Perez Oxlaj

Mayan Spiritual Leader

MAYAN CERAMIC VASE

we are *all* brothers and sisters,
we *all* have equal value, like flowers of one garden.

Injustice sprouts from the deep roots of distrust and intolerance found in the human mind. People of religion in the 21st century must work hard to overcome the negative forces of the human mind. Where ethnic conflicts break out, there exists a clash of interest in politics, ethnic bias, culture, and things of that nature. We have seen in some cases that rulers of various peoples intentionally used religion to start conflicts. However, we should not let religions cause killing since the primary role of religion is to support people in peace and security. We are from different religious organizations and different sects. Our religious doctrines may differ and we observe ceremonies in accordance with different traditions. We have, however, the same basic ground of searching for peace and compassion. It is at this point that we can develop mutual understanding through friendship, from which I believe we can transform conflicts into compassion. This is the very task that Buddha urges people of faith to embrace. We must take responsibility for every man and woman living in the world of today as well as those of tomorrow.

Venerable Eshin Watanabe
Patriarch of Tendai Buddhism

WE CAN TRANSFORM CONFLICTS INTO COMPASSION.

this is the
very task that
Buddha urges
people of faith
to embrace.
we must take
responsibility
for every man
and woman
living in the world
of today
as well as those
of tomorrow.

For me, practicing Islam means spreading justice, struggling against oppression, inviting love, refusing hatred, appealing for peace, standing against wars, looking for tolerance, and fighting discrimination in order to integrate human beings without any distinction.

As Allah says in the Holy Koran, there shall not be any distinction between white and black, rich and poor, or strong and weak: "O mankind! We created you from a single (pair) of male and female, and made you into nations and tribes, that ye may know each other (not that ye may despise each other). Verily the most honored of you in the sight of Allah is (he who is) the most righteous of you. And Allah has full knowledge and is well acquainted (with all things)." (Sura Al-Hojorat, Verse 13) The Holy Prophet Mohammed also said: "People are equal like the teeth of a comb and there is no difference between an Arabic man and a non-Arabic one except by righteousness."

As the Holy Koran says, a true Muslim has tolerance and believes in the previous Prophets and the holy books that Allah revealed upon them: "Say ye: we believe in Allah, and the revelation given to us, and to Abraham, Ismail, Isaac, Jacob, and all the tribes. And, to that given to Moses and Jesus, and that given to (all) prophets from their Lord. We make no difference between one and another of them. And, we bow to Allah (in Islam)." (Sura Al-Baquara, Verse 134)

His Excellency Sheikh Fawzi al-Zafzaf

Wakil al-Azhar

PATTERNED TILE, MOROCCO

"People are equal like the teeth of a comb
AND THERE IS NO DIFFERENCE
between an Arabic man and a non-Arabic one
except by righteousness."

APPENDIX
Biographies of Religious Leaders

HIS HOLINESS PATRIARCH ALEXY II OF MOSCOW AND ALL RUSSIA is the 15th primate of the Russian Orthodox Church since the patriarchal office was established in Russia in 1589. He has published over 450 articles, addresses and papers on theology, church history, peacemaking and ecumenical and other issues in the ecclesiastical and secular press in Russia and abroad. Patriarch Alexy considers practical cooperation among various Christian confessions in alleviating the needs of the world today to be a Christian duty and the way to the fulfillment of Christ's commandment of unity.

HER HOLINESS SRI SRI MATA AMRITANANDAMAYI DEVI has helped to alleviate human suffering and poverty by her humanitarian work. She has inspired an extensive list of charitable institutions—hospitals, orphanages, schools, and monthly stipends to 50,000 destitute women. Though born into the Hindu faith, Amma steadfastly supports all great religions, encouraging adherents to go deeper in their own traditional path. Regarding religious rivalry, Amma says, "Hundreds fight and die in the name of religion, but only a few realize that religion is something that needs to be lived."

HIS HOLINESS ARAM I is the Catholicos of the Great House of Cilicia in the Armenian Apostolic Orthodox Church and the Moderator of the Central Committee of the World Council of Churches. Born in Lebanon in 1947, Aram Keshishian holds a doctorate in theology from Fordham University, New York, and has completed a postgraduate course at the Ecumenical Institute in Bossey, Switzerland. He was ordained to the priesthood in 1968. Aram I is the author of several books, including *The Witness of the Armenian Church* and *Christian Witness at the Crossroads in the Middle East*.

HIS ALL HOLINESS ECUMENICAL PATRIARCH BARTHOLOMEW is the 270th successor to the Apostle Andrew and spiritual leader of 300 million Orthodox Christians worldwide. Since ascending the Ecumenical Throne on November 2nd, 1991, he has tirelessly pursued the vision of his enthronement message—spiritual revival, Orthodox unity, Christian reconciliation, interfaith tolerance and coexistence, protection of the environment, and a world united in peace, justice, solidarity, and love.

HIS EXCELLENCY ALHAJI ADO BAYERO was born at Kano, capital of Kano State of Nigeria on the 15th of June, 1930. He is the son of the Emir of Kano Alhaji Abdullahi Bayero. He started Quranic School beginning in 1935. In 1958 he became a member of the Northern House of Assembly for Kano Central. He became Chief of N.A. Police in 1959 and was made Ambassador Extraordinary and Plenipotentiary to Senegal in 1962. In 1963 he became Emir of Kano. He was made Chancellor of the University of Maiduguri in 1988.

HIS GRACE REVEREND GEORGE CAREY is the 103rd Archbishop of Canterbury, enthroned on April 19, 1991. Dr Carey is the author of fourteen books on theological issues, including our understanding of Christ, ecumenism, relationships with the Roman Catholic Church, and the existence of God. He has also contributed articles and reviews to many journals and periodicals. He has introduced and conducted a series of teaching missions, seeking to deepen faith and knowledge in deaneries and parishes. He has continued these in the Canterbury diocese since he became Archbishop in March 1991.

HIS EXCELLENCY DR. MUSTAFA CERIC has been a strong voice for both the recognition of and forgiveness for the crimes against humanity that have occurred in the Balkans. He is also deeply concerned with creating a stronger, peaceful relationship between Islam and the West. In his words, "The threat is not in Islam but in our spiritual disability to meet universal moral demands; evil is not in the West but in our cultural insecurity. It is time that Islam be seen as a spiritual blessing in the West, and the West be seen as a call for an intellectual awakening in the Muslim East."

HIS HOLINESS SWAMI DAYANANDA SARASWATI is a teacher of Vedanta and an eminent scholar of Sanskrit. He was born into a traditional Hindu family in 1930 in a village in Thanjavur District, the cultural hub of Tamilnadu. Swamiji has established three institutions of learning and culture, two in India and one in the USA. Swamiji has achieved international recognition as one of the foremost authorities on Vedanta. He has conducted many courses and delivered lectures throughout the world, and through this medium has made the wisdom of the Upanishads available to modern seekers.

HIS EXCELLENCY MUFTI RAVIL GAINUTDIN was born in the Russian Federation, in Kazan in 1959. From 1991 until 1994 he was president of the Islamic Center of Russia's European regions. In 1994 he was elected mufti, and is currently the chairman of the Russian mufties council. Ravil Gainutdin is the author of several books on theology, and a member of several Academies (International Academy of Euroasian science, International Slavyan Academy, etc.). He organized Russia's Interconfessional council and is member of the Russian Presidents Council. He was awarded the Order of Friendship for his activity.

HONORABLE ELA GANDHI, Mahatma Gandhi's granddaughter, was born in 1950 in KwaZulu Natal province. She has served on Parliamentary Committees in Judiciary and Legal Systems, Welfare and Public Enterprise. She was executive member of the Natal Organization for Women from its inception to 1991 and has worked with several child and family welfare societies. She has worked on a volunteer basis in deprived communities assisting in economic development, combating violence, and supporting environmental concerns.

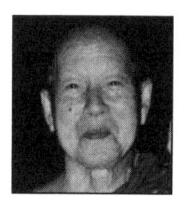

VENERABLE SAMDECH PREAH MAHA GHOSANANDA is the Supreme Patriarch of Buddhism for the Kingdom of Cambodia and has been nominated for the Nobel Peace Prize five times. He is famous for leading peace marches throughout Cambodia and former Khmer Rouge territory (where 17 of his brothers and sisters were killed) as a form of active reconciliation. He has been a scholar at Nalanda Buddhist University in India, and speaks 15 languages. Maha Ghosananda is widely recognized for his efforts to safely remove the land mines which plague Southeast Asia.

REVEREND BILLY GRAHAM has preached the Gospel to more people in live audiences than anyone else in history—over 210 million people in more than 185 countries and territories—through various meetings, including Mission World and Global Mission. Hundreds of millions more have been reached through television, video, and film. Today, at age 82, Billy Graham and his ministry are known around the globe. He has preached in remote African villages and in the heart of New York City, and those to whom he has ministered have ranged from heads of state to the simple-living bushmen of Australia and the wandering tribes of the Middle East.

HIS HOLINESS TENZIN GYATSO the Dalai Lama, was born Lhamo Dhondrub on July 6th, 1935, in the small village of Taktser in northeastern Tibet and recognized by age two as the 14th incarnation of the Dalai Lama. He is the leader of Tibetan Buddhism, a Buddhist monk, and a prolific scholar. He is respected internationally as an environmentalist and as an advocate of compassion and personal responsibility. He inspires people worldwide with his grace, compassion, and ability to embrace the integrity of other faith traditions. He is the most traveled Dalai Lama in history and, in 1989, was awarded the Nobel Prize for peace.

REVEREND JESSE JACKSON is the son of impoverished parents from South Carolina. Reverend Jackson graduated Chicago Theological Seminary in 1965 and was ordained a Baptist minister in 1968. During the early years of his ministry, he was a close associate of the Reverend Martin Luther King, and following Dr. King's assassination, became one of the leaders of the Southern Christian Leadership Conference. The Executive Director of Operation Breadbasket, the Reverend Jackson founded and led Operation PUSH (People United to Save Humanity) and was the organizer of the Rainbow Coalition.

HER HOLINESS DADI JANKI is the co-administrative head of the Brahma Kumaris World Spiritual University. She has dedicated her life to the principles and practices of the Brahma Kumaris. Her decision came as an inspiration from the founder, Brahma Baba, with whom she shared a vision of a world of peace and purity. She embodies the passion to experience the essence of spiritual truths within herself and the power of bringing this essence into practical action.

HIS HOLINESS SHRI JAYENDRA SARASWATI is the 69th pontiff of the Kanchi Kamakoti Peetam. This religious seat was established by Adi Sankara, one of India's greatest philosophers and spiritualists. His Holiness was initiated as a sannyasi (renunciate) in 1954 and was under the tutelage of his guru, the 68th pontiff. He has guided the institution in its traditional role and has boldly moved into new areas of volunteerism and self help, stressing the need to assist the less fortunate among us. His pioneering vision has led to the opening of much needed schools, colleges, hospitals, and religious study centers.

HONORABLE CORETTA SCOTT KING was born in Alabama in 1927. Coretta Scott King is the widow of the Reverend Martin Luther King. Following his death she assumed a critical role in the leadership of the civil rights movement and has been at the forefront of the campaign to deal with issues of poverty and race in America. She is the founder of the Martin Luther King Jr. Center for Nonviolent Social Change.

HIS EXCELLENCY SHEIKH AHMED KUFTARO, the Grand Mufti of Syria, Head of the Supreme Council of Fatwa, was born in Damascus in 1915, son of Muhammad Amin Kuftaro (1875-1938), a great scholar of his day. Since 1938, at the death of his father, he has been the head of the Naqshabandi order, preaching and calling for the pursuit of universal knowledge, freedom of religion, interfaith cooperation, and more recently, for the protection of the global environment. The major commitment of Sheikh Ahmad Kuftaro throughout his life has been to interfaith understanding and cooperation in pursuit of peace.

THE MOST REVEREND IZU KUDO was born in 1922 in Aomori prefecture, Japan. He became the Chief Priest of Takayama Inari Jinja in 1953, and in 1973 he became the Director of the Aomori Prefectural Office of the Association of Shinto Shrines. In 1998 he assumed the post of the President of the Association of Shinto Shrines.

CHIEF RABBI ISRAEL MEIR LAU was born in 1937 in Pyotrekov, Poland. A survivor of the Buchenwald concentration camp, he lost both of his parents in the Holocaust. In 1946 he immigrated to Israel and then studied at three yeshivas: Kol Torah in Jerusalem, Knesset Hizkiya in Zichron Ya'akov, and Ponovitz in Bnei Brak. In 1971 he was ordained as a rabbi. In 1993 he was elected Ashkenazi Chief Rabbi of Israel. Rabbi Lau's publications include "Yahadut - Halacha Le'maase" (1975) on the practice of Judaism, and "Yachel Israel" (1993), two volumes on medicine, ethics, and Jewish customs.

DR. ALBERT LINCOLN is the highest ranking officer of the Baha'i International Community, a worldwide religious movement accredited to the United Nations as an international non-governmental organization with consultative status. He reports directly to the Universal House of Justice, the elected governing body ordained in the Baha'i Sacred Writings, and serves as its chief diplomatic representative in dealings with royalty, heads of state and government, as well as leaders of other religions. A graduate of Harvard College and the University of Chicago Law School, he speaks four languages.

HER HOLINESS SRI DAYA MATA is the foremost living disciple of Paramahansa Yogananda (1893-1952). Designated by him to lead his spiritual and humanitarian work, she has served since 1955 as president and sanghamata of the international society he founded, Self-Realization Fellowship/Yogoda Satsanga Society of India. One of the first women in history to be appointed head of a worldwide religious movement, she has inspired people of all faiths and from all walks of life through her talks, writings, and recordings.

REVEREND DR. VASHTI MURPHY MCKENZIE, former pastor of Payne Memorial AME Church in Baltimore, was recently elected its 117th bishop. Bishop McKenzie's election on July 11, 2000 and subsequent consecration on July 12, 2000, represented the first time in the 213-year history of the church that a woman has obtained the level of the episcopacy. Dr. McKenzie has traveled considerably and continues to do so across the United States and beyond. Her preaching ministry has taken her from Alaska to Bermuda, Europe, and the Caribbean. She continues to serve as preacher, revivalist, keynote speaker, worship, and seminar leader.

REVEREND NICHIKO NIWANO was born on November 15, 1906. He founded Rissho Kosei-kai in 1938 and was the organization's president until 1991. He is an honorary president of the World Conference on Religion and Peace, the International Association for Religious Freedom, and the Niwano Peace Foundation, and honorary chairman of Shinshuren (Federation of New Religious Organizations of Japan). His works published in English include *Buddhism for Today*, *Invisible Eyelashes*, *A Buddhist Approach to Peace*, and many others.

HIS GRACE REVEREND NJONGONKULU NDUNGANE was born in Kokstad, South Africa, on April 2, 1941. During March 1960, Njongonkulu was involved in Pass law Demonstrations while a student at the University of Cape Town. Beginning in August 1963 he served a three-year sentence on Robben Island as a political prisoner. He received a Bachelor of Divinity, Honours at King's College, London in June 1978. In June 1979 he completed his Masters of Theology in Christian Ethics, with King's College, London. He has written many essays and made numerous contributions to books.

HIS EXCELLENCY DASTUR DR. JEHANGIR OSHIDARI is Vice-President of the Iranian Mobed Council, which sets policy on questions of religion, philosophy and ritual. He was born in Tehran in 1920 and holds a Ph.D. in Veterinary Science. He retired from his profession about five years ago. He is the author of two books in Farsi: *Encyclopedia of Zarthusti History*, and *History of Zoroastrians in Iran*. He also published memoirs of Arbab Kaikhosrow Shahrokh, who was an influential member of the Iranian Majlis during 1920-21. His message to Zarthustis in North America is to preserve "Unity."

HIS HOLINESS POPE JOHN PAUL II formerly known as Karol Wojtyla, was born on May 18, 1920 at Wadowice, Poland. For many years Karol believed God was calling him to the priesthood, and after two near fatal accidents, he responded to God's call. He studied secretly during the German occupation of Poland, and was ordained to the priesthood on November 1, 1946. On October 16, 1978, Archbishop Wojtyla became the first non-Italian pope since Hadrian VI (1522-3). Pope John Paul II is the most traveled pope in the history of the papacy, having visited nearly every country in the world.

HIS HOLINESS ABUNE PAULOS was born within the territorial confines of the Monastery of Abba Gerima, Adewa, Tigray on Tekemt 25, 1930 (November 3, 1938). He was consecrated a bishop in September, 1975 by His Holiness Abune Tewolflos, the Second Patriarch of Ethiopia. He was enthroned as the Fifth Patriarch of the Ethiopian Orthodox Church on July 5, 1992. Since his enthronement, he has exerted great effort to intensify the dissemination of the Gospel, strengthen the administration of the Church, and broaden the scope of the international relations of the Church.

THE REVEREND DR. KONRAD RAISER is the fifth General Secretary of the World Council of Churches (WCC), founded in 1948. The WCC has approximately 400 million Christian members represented through more than 330 churches, denominations, and fellowships in 100 countries and territories throughout the world. Founded in 1948, WCC works toward the universal calling, "one human family in justice and peace." Reverend Raiser's publications include "To Be the Church, Challenges and Hope for a New Millennium" (1997), and "Ecumenism in Transition" (1991).

84 | SACRED RIGHTS

CHIEF RABBI JONATHAN SACKS has been Chief Rabbi of the United Hebrew Congregations of the Commonwealth since September 1, 1991, the sixth incumbent since 1845. At his installation as Chief Rabbi, Professor Sacks set out his vision of a reinvigorated Anglo-Jewry, launching it with a Decade of Jewish Renewal, followed by a series of innovative communal projects. In 1995, he received the Jerusalem Prize for his contribution to Diaspora Jewish life. A notably gifted communicator, he is a frequent contributor to radio, television, and the national press. He is the author of eleven books.

VENERABLE SHENG-YEN was born in Shanghai, ordained at 13, and at 28 had a deep spiritual experience after which he completed a six-year solitary retreat. Within the Lin-Chi lineage, Master Sheng-yen is a 62nd generation descendant of Master Lin-Chi (ca. 866) and is widely recognized as one of the foremost teachers in contemporary Buddhism. The impact of his teachings, social engagement, writings, and personal example has been felt throughout the Far East and increasingly in the West. Master Sheng-yen is also the founder of the Chung-Hwa Institute of Buddhist Studies in Taipei.

HIS EXCELLENCY DR. L. M. SINGHVI is a Jain and Indic scholar and leader. He is a member of the upper house of Parliament of India, and a Chair on the Indian National Committee for the Abolition of the Death Penalty. He was the past president of the Asian Human Rights Conference. As High Commissioner (ambassador) of India to the United Kingdom, he wrote the final version of the Jain Declaration on Nature.

RABBI ADIN STEINSALTZ was born in Jerusalem and is a leading scholar in the world of Talmud, having worked for the past decade on an edition of that classic work that is intended for the contemporary student. An original thinker, he has written various works that have been translated into many languages. Dr. Steinsaltz has been a member of the Institute of Advanced Study at Princeton and has been involved in interfaith activities for the realization of world peace.

CHIEF JAKE SWAMP (Wolf Clan of the Mohawk Nation, Six Nations Iroquois Confederacy) is a respected spiritual leader who has participated in crucial Native American struggles. These include the 1970 takeover of the Bureau of Indian Affairs office in Washington DC, settlement talks after the Wounded Knee occupation, and the 1978 Longest Walk. In addition to sitting on the grand council of the Iroquois Confederacy, he served as Director of the Akwesasne Freedom School. For the past two decades, he has traveled extensively, planting trees for peace and spreading a powerful message of peace and environmental education.

HIS EXCELLENCY DR. ABDULLAH BIN ABDUL MUHSIN AL TURKI is Secretary-General of the Muslim World League and, as such, is responsible for the implementation of decisions and recommendations adopted by the Constituent Council (the policy-making body). He is responsible for the administrative and financial structure of the League and represents the link between the League and various organizations around the world. Dr. Turki also oversees the day-to-day activities of the League.

CIRILO ALEJANDRO PEREZ OXLAJ was born February 26, 1929. His Maya name is Wakatel Utiw, which means "Wandering Wolf." He is the Voice of the Jungle and the Messenger of the Mayas by mandate of the Invisible Beings. In his youth he was a land worker, a laborer, a tailor, and concurrently a medicine man. He is an expert in reading glyphs. He has lectured on the Maya Tradition at various universities in the US, Mexico, Central and South America as well as in Europe. He is a member of the Maya National Counsel of Elders of Guatemala.

THE MOST VENERABLE ESHIN WATANABE is the Patriarch of the Tendai school of Buddhism in Mt. Hiei, Japan. The Tendai school is the cradle of Japanese Buddhism and represents a common historical lineage for all the various schools of Japanese Buddhism. He is renowned for his Buddhist scholarship throughout Japan and internationally.

HIS EXCELLENCY SHEIKH FAWZI AL-ZAFZAF is the Wakil of al-Azhar, the 1,000-year old institution in Cairo, Egypt that serves as the unequivocal religious and moral authority of the Sunni Muslim world. Additionally, Sheikh Zafzaf is President of the Permanent Committee of al-Azhar for Dialogue with the Monotheistic Religions, an official al-Azhar organization created in 1997 to promote dialogue, fraternity, solidarity, cooperation, justice, and peace. He also serves as the Secretary General of al-Azhar's High Islamic Council, and is a member of the Academy of Islamic Research.

THANK YOU

Special thanks are due to Her Excellency Mary Robinson for help in making this book possible, as well as to Mr. Jyoti Shankar Singh, Executive Coordinator, World Conference Against Racism. We also wish to acknowledge the following: Barbara Berasi, Zena Devres, Daniel Dolgin, David Finn, Indira Gumarover, Joshua M. Greene, Bawa Jain, Dena Merriam, Tanya Serdivk, Susan Slack, Kavita Shah, Astrid Stuckelberger, and the many religious and spiritual leaders who graciously provided statements. Acknowledgements are due, as well, to the staff in the Office of the High Commissioner for Human Rights who also assisted with this project.

A special thanks to the co-sponsers of the book; The Modi Foundation, The Museum of World Religions and Namdhari International Trust.